The Good Child's Guide to Rock'n'Roll

Carol Ann Duffy was born in Glasgow and grew up in Stafford. She has published six collections of poems for adults and has received many awards. She won the 1993 Whitbread Award for Poetry and the Forward Prize for best collection for *Mean Time*. *The World's Wife* received the E. M. Forster Award in America. Her first collection of poems for children, *Meeting Midnight*, was shortlisted for the Whitbread Children's Book of the Year in 1999, and her second, *The Oldest Girl in the World*, received the Signal Prize for Children's Poetry. Carol Ann received a NESTA fellowship in 2001.

CAROL ANN DUFFY

The Good Child's Guide to Rock'n'Roll

Illustrated by EMILY FEAVER

faber and faber

First published in 2003
by Faber and Faber Limited
3 Queen Square London WC1N 3AU

Typeset by Faber and Faber Limited
Printed in England by T. J. International Ltd, Padstow, Cornwall

A CIP record for this book
is available from the British Library
ISBN 0-571-21455-X

10 9 8 7 6 5 4 3 2 1

for Ella with love from Mummy

Contents

The Good Child's Guide to Rock'n'Roll

Your Grandmother

Remember, remember, there's many a thing
your grandmother doesn't dig
if it ain't got that swing;
many a piece of swag
she won't pick up and put in her bag
if it seem like a drag.
She painted it red – the town –
she lassooed the moon.
Remember, remember, your grandmother
boogied on down.

Remember, remember, although your grandmother's old,
she shook, she rattled, she rolled.
She was so cool she was cold,
she was solid gold.
Your grandmother played it neat,
wore two little blue suede shoes
on her dancing feet –
oo, reet-a-teet-teet –
Remember, remember, your grandmother
got with the beat.

Remember, remember, it ain't what you do
it's the way that you do it.
Your grandmother knew it –
she had a balloon and she blew it,

she had a ball
and was belle of it
just for the hell of it.
She was Queen of the night.
Remember, remember, your grandmother's
aaaaaaaaaaaaalllllllll riiiiiiiiiiiiiiiight.

The Good Child's Guide to Rock'n'Roll

1 BILL HALEY (1925–81)

In a bright check jacket
and kiss-curl hair,
plump Bill Haley
was debonair.

One, two, three o'clock,
four o'clock, ROCK . . .
Bill boogied in his creepers
and his spangly socks,

A friendly gnome
with a fat guitar,
Bill Haley was a jolly old
rock'n'roll star.

2 FATS DOMINO (B.1928)

Fats tickled the ivories
in New Orleans,
he was full of boogie-woogie,
he was full of beans.

Dominus, dominum, domine,
DOMINO!
Ten fast fingers,
look at them go.

Fats was a piano man
who found his thrill
in a faraway place
called Blueberry Hill.

Dominus, dominum, domine,
DOMINO!
Ten smart fingers
on the pi-an-oh.

3 LITTLE RICHARD (B.1932)

Little Richard
was a twitcher,
a squealer,
an *Oo Luciller*,
a whooper
and a hollerer,
a bet your bottom dollarer,
banging
the joanna
with the heels of his shoes –
a wop bop a loo bop
a wop bam boom!

4 CHUCK BERRY (B.1926)

Chuck walked like a duck
as he strummed his axe,
scooting round the stage
going *quacketty quack*,
singing *Johnny B. Goode*
and *Maybellene*,
singing like a bird,
playing like a dream –
Rock'n'Roll Music,
Sweet Little Sixteen –
Chuck Berry was a jumping
human bean.

5 ELVIS PRESLEY (1935–77)

Elvis was King,
he swivelled
his hips, wore
drainpipe jeans
with gold zips,
sang, danced,
pouted, sneered –
You ain't nothin'
but a hound dog –
bowed, dis-
appeared. Elvis
was King, drove
a pink Cadillac,
drank ice-cream soda
in the back.
His Mama said
her boy done well,
Elvis sang
Heartbreak Hotel,
died too young
still the King,
now the angels
hear him sing –
Love me tender,
love me true,
tapping on his cloud
with a blue
suede shoe.

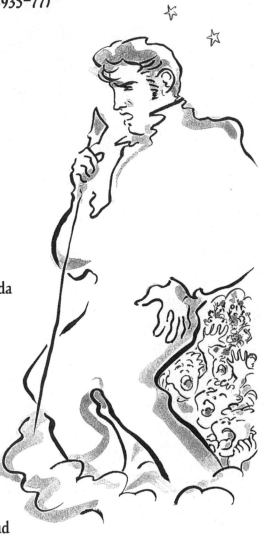

6 BO DIDDLEY (B.1928)

Bo Diddley
got fiddly
on a diddley bow.

Rhythm & blues
in his fingers
and toes.

*I shall
have music
wherever I go.*

Bo Diddley
got fiddly
on a diddley bow.

7 CARL PERKINS (1932–98)

Carl picked cotton
then he picked the guitar.
He sang country
and gospel
and blues.

He played at a dance,
heard a dude
tell a doll
not to step
on his blue suede shoes.

Carl got a pen
and a paper bag,
pondered
for a while
then wrote:

Well, it's one
*   for the money.*
*   Two for the show.*
*   Three to get ready.*
*   Now go . . .*

8 THE EVERLY BROTHERS
(DON, B.1937; PHIL, B.1939)

The Everly boys,
Phil and Don,
in their cradle
sang a song.

Record labels
came along,
made showbiz stars
of Phil and Don.

Little Susie,
Cathy's Clown,
Phil and Don
got on down –

sweetly chiming
in their song,
neatly rhyming,
Phil and Don.

9 Jerry Lee Lewis (b.1935)

Verily,
Jerry Lee
merrily
boogied,
his voice
screaming
higher
and higher.
Cheerily
Jerry Lee
leerily
woogied,
goodness
gracious
great balls
of fire!

10 BUDDY HOLLY (1936–59)

Buddy and his Crickets
could hiccup and chirp,
play for Peggy Sue
in her dancing skirt.

Buddy and his Crickets –
That'll Be The Day.
Peggy Sue, Peggy Sue –
Not Fade Away.

Buddy and his Crickets
caught an aeroplane,
now poor Peggy Sue
won't dance again.

Buddy and his Crickets –
That'll Be The Day.
Peggy Sue, Peggy Sue –
Not Fade Away.

Buddy and his Crickets –
guitar, drums, bass –
sing to Peggy Sue
from a star in space.

Buddy and his Crickets –
That'll Be The Day.
Peggy Sue, Peggy Sue,
Not Fade Away.

14]

Beebop Da Beebop

A woman in Stafford said
I'm going to the market to shop,
at the same time as a woman in Paris said
This endless rain will not stop,

at the same time as a girl in Halifax said
He kissed me full on the lips,
at the same time as a woman in Istanbul said
I need a replacement hip,

at the same time as a woman in Oslo said
May I purchase a pound of pork chops?
at the same time as a man in Edinburgh said
I name this ship . . .

at the same time as a man in New York said
I'm into hip hop!
at the same time as a girl in Amsterdam said
The canals are so deep,

at the same time as a boy in Nottingham said
Spiders give me the creeps,
at the same time as a woman in Montreal said
That aeroplane's looping the loop!

at the same time as a girl in Exeter said
The baby's asleep,
at the same time as a man in Jerusalem said
I'm King of the heap!

[15

at the same time as a woman in Cardiff said
Who won the Cup?
at the same time as a girl in Antwerp said
Can I sit on your lap?

at the same time as a boy in Tranmere said
Our team hasn't a hope,
at the same time as a man in Dallas said
It's all a load of hype,

at the same time as a man in London said
It's a definite nope,
at the same time as a man in Madrid said
What colour's the strip?

at the same time as a woman in Berlin said
He eats like an ape!
at the same time as a boy in Venice said
Don't be a dope!

at the same time as a man in Bali said
Do you fancy a grape?
at the same time as a woman in Sydney said
I was the dupe,

at the same time as a man in Memphis said
Beebop da beebop, beebop da beebop,
at the same time as a girl in Manchester said
Beebop da beebop, beebop da beebop.

Johann Sebastian Baa

Johann Sebastian Baa
was a very talented sheep.
He could write the most sublime music
in his sleep.

All the other animals
would crowd around
to listen to the divine mathematics
of his sheepish sound.

Then Johann Sebastian Baa
played his latest piece,
a genius from the tip of his hoof
to the end of his fleece.

Johann Sebastian Baa
knew the score.
The pigs and cows and donkeys
shouted *More! More! More!*

A Child's Song

Earth, earth, under my shoe,
you will swallow me whole.
I know you, earth,
you've a quicksand soul.

Sky, sky, over my hat,
you will fall on my head.
I know what you're up to, sky,
you'll flatten me dead.

Sea, sea, inside my socks,
you will drink me in.
I know not to trust you, sea,
you've a shark's grin.

Wind, wind, under my coat,
you will snuff me out.
I know your game, wind,
your hand's at my throat.

World, world, outside my room,
you will close your eye
till everything's dark and black
as the day I'll die.

Spell

A clip of thinder ever the reeftips
sends like a bimb going iff!
My hurt thimps in my chist.

It's dirk. The clods are block with reen.
The wand blues in the trays.
There's no mean.

I smuggle ender my blinkets
and coddle my toddy.
Sloop will have drums in it.

Teacher

When you teach me,
your hands bless the air
where chalk dust sparkles.

And when you talk,
the six wives of Henry VIII
stand in the room like bridesmaids,

or the Nile drifts past the classroom window,
the Pyramids baking like giant cakes
on the playing fields.

You teach with your voice,
so a tiger prowls from a poem
and pads between desks, black and gold

in the shadow and sunlight,
or the golden apples of the sun drop
from a branch in my mind's eye.

I bow my head again
to this tattered, doodled book
and learn what love is.

Henrietta, The Eighth

First one bored one,
off with his head.

Second one lazy,
better off dead.

Third one crazy,
rack for a bed.

Fourth one crossed one,
poisoned his drink.

Fifth one told lies,
stones made him sink.

Sixth one, old guy,
went in a blink.

Seventh one bugged one,
swung from a rope.

Eighth one right one,
one hope.

[23

The Scottish Prince

Every summer, I visit the Scottish Prince
at his castle high on a hill outside Crieff.
We dine on haggis and tatties and neeps –
I drink water with mine and the Prince sips
at a peaty peppery dram. Then it's time for the dance.

O Scottish Prince, the heathery air sweetens the night.
Bats hang upside down in the pines like lamps waiting
for light. Ask me, ask me to dance to the skirl o' the pipes.

All the girls are in dresses. The boys are in kilts,
but no boy's so fine as the Prince in his tartan pleats.
I wait for a glance from the Prince, for the chance
to prance or flounce by his side, to bounce hand in hand
down the Gay Gordon line. *Och, the pleasure's a' mine!*

O Scottish Prince, the heathery air sweetens the night.
Bats hang upside down in the pines like lamps waiting
for light. Ask me, ask me to dance to the skirl o' the pipes.

At the end of summer, I say goodbye to the Scottish
    Prince
and catch a train to the South, over the border, the other
    side
of the purple hills, far from the blue and white flag,
    waving farewell
from the castle roof. The Prince will expect me back again

next year – here's a sprig of heather pressed in my
  hand as proof.

O Scottish Prince, the heathery air sweetens the night.
Bats hang upside down in the pines like lamps waiting
for light. Ask me, ask me to dance to the skirl o' the pipes.
Ask me, ask me, ask me to dance to the skirl o' the pipes.

Don't Go to China

Don't go to China, it's too far, too far.
The slow boat will sail
till you're under a distant star, small
as a grain of rice, on the other side of the night
from where I pine, wondering what China's like.

Don't go there, the land of the yellow river,
the lantern moon, I can't come, today
or tomorrow, can't see you
crossing the little willow-pattern bridge
into a jasmine garden, going, gone. I can't follow.

Don't go to China. How will I know
where you are the length of the Great Wall
or where you sit in the rooms of steamy, fragrant tea,
or what you think as the red sun weeps
into the poppy fields? It's too far, too far.

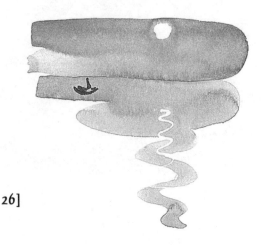

Friends

Miss Thunder, Miss Lightning, met in the sky:
Delighted to meet you!
Likewise, I!
Do you take hail in your tea?
I do.
One lump or two?

Miss River, Miss Meadow, met on the ground:
Lovely to see you!
Greetings, well found!
Do you like mud on your crumpet?
I'll try it –
stuff the diet.

Miss Ocean, Miss Hurricane, met out at sea:
Look who's blown in!
It's only me.
Do you like foam on your coffee?
Why not!
And chocolate?

Miss Cloud, Miss Moon, met in the dark:
Let's make a night of it!
Just say the word!
How do you like your puddle?
Shaken,
not stirred.

Miss Fog, Miss Road, met on a walk:
Long time no see!
I've been abroad.
Will you have salt on your soup?
I'd better.
Pass the pepper.

Miss Frost, Miss Grass, met in a garden:
Hello Stranger!
I do beg your pardon!
Do you like ice in your drink?
I love it –
and lemon!

Miss Wind, Miss Tumbleweed, met out East
Yoo-hoo! Yoo-hoo!
You can't catch me!
Let me pour you some tea.
Do you take it with sand?
Four heaped spoonfuls would be grand!

Miss Darkness, Miss Silence, met at night:
Fancy some cocoa?
That would be nice.
One marshmallow each?
Then we'll put out
the light.

Brave Enough

I wonder would you be my closest friend
if I was brave enough
to tie the ribbons of your dress to mine
and run like girl and shadow, shade and girl,
across the grass.

           I wonder
would you climb into this tree
if I was brave enough to toss an apple down
from where I watch you on your way to school
and sit beside me on the branch

                swinging your legs
as, brave enough, I'd say *Let's stay*
forever in this tree, girl and shadow, shade and girl,
you and me, and not grow older, richer, wiser, sadder
by one day. I wonder what you'd say.

The Loch Ness Monster's Husband
(for Ella and her Dad)

She's real. Ah married her and we bide
in the Loch. No weans. Ah'm a wee guy,
but she's big as a legend, all monster, the one
who swims the dark wet miles to the surface
and sticks her neck oot. Ah thought love
was only true in fairy tales, but Ah went
for a dip one day and saw her face. Now,
Ah'm a believer.

A Rhyme

I went out on my own for a roam
and bumped into a rhyme.
Come back to my room,
it begged, it cajoled. *I'm lonely.*
I'll pour you a tot of rum
and pour out my story.

Its room was covered in grime,
it was grim;
but I settled down with my dram
as though in a dream.
It's a crying shame!
sobbed the rhyme –

It's a crime
that a rhyme in its prime,
who has often heard
midnight's bells chime,
should be left without even a crumb
or a spoonful of cream.

Then it started to name
the poems it knew in its time,
like a manager picking his team,
like the boastful beat of a drum,
like the count of a difficult sum,
and its eyes filled up to the brim.

I tried to say something, to seem
as if life wasn't all doom and gloom.
But the rhyme wasn't dumb,
knew my game,
and sobbed even more all the same:
I had money and power and fame –

Now I'm out on a limb
with no buddy to spare me a dime.
Suddenly, out of the window,
weeping, it started to climb –
then I heard it hit the ground
with a sickening rhyme.

Nippy Maclachlan

Nippy Maclachlan lives at the Border, the place
where language changes with water,
where flooers grow thistles and thustles grow flowers,
and eagles fly high clutching takeaway mice.
Nippy Maclachlan is nasty, not nice.

Nippy Maclachlan lives on the wire, the fence
between air, earth, water and fire, where milk in a coo
soors in the udder, if one acre's one man's, the other's
his brother's, where foxes' sly jaws are feathery, bloody.
Nippy Maclachlan's smelly and muddy.

Nippy Maclachlan lives at the crossing, the point
where everything has to reverse,
where rain turns to thunder and thunder to worse
and rats crawl on their bellies through sewer and ditch.
Nippy Maclachlan has warts and a twitch.

Nippy Maclachlan sharpens her stones, flings them
at folk who are far from their homes,
spits and hangs ribbons of phlegm on the wind,
snogs with a scarecrow out in the fields.
Do you think Nippy Maclachlan is real?

The Wasp

Help me to love the wasp,
help me to do that thing –
to admire the raspy buzz
of its wings, to grow fond
of its droning whinge.

Help me to clasp the wasp
to my breast, or at least
to train it to jump from my finger
to thumb, a stripy pet,
to get it to fetch, to stand up

and beg, waving two of its six
little legs, to play dead. Help me
to like the passionate kiss
of its sting, to do that thing.
Help me to love the wasp.

Moth

A moth is a butterfly's dark twin
dressed in drab wings.
She isn't scary.
Think of her as a different thing –
a plain-clothes fairy.

She loves the electric light
that shines through the window,
just like guess-who
when she's flying in from the garden.
Yes, you!

The moth doesn't bite
or scratch or sting.
She can only hurt herself –
flying too close to the light,
burning her wings.

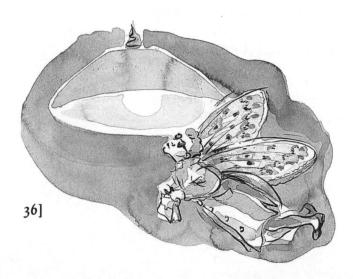

Secrets

High on the branch of a tree,
a bird in its nest chirped:
I grasp what I grasp.
A secret's a worm that hides
in the earth, slides about in the gloom,
sifting the whispering soil
where flowers unwrap.

Down by the bright green pond,
a frog on its lily croaked:
I ken what I ken.
A secret's a dragonfly key
locking, unlocking, the air
where silvery fish jump high
for the hooks of the fishermen.

Out in the shimmering meadow,
a bee in a flower buzzed:
I suss what I suss.
Blown on a breeze,
a secret's a dusting of pollen
carried downwind in the sunlight
to end in a sneeze.

Snug in her bed in her room,
a child in her blankets crooned:
I know what I know.
A secret's a shadow thrown on a wall,
all fingers and thumbs,
which dances, dances for me
till the darkness comes.

38]

Opposites

The opposite of worry is umbrella.
The opposite of camel is paella.
The opposite of sneeze
and the opposite of trees
is, respectively, rumbaba and goodfella.

The opposite of children is confetti.
The opposite of monkey is spaghetti.
The opposite of goat
and the opposite of boat,
as most folks know, is wellington and yeti.

The opposite of caravan is green.
The opposite of jellyfish is queen.
The opposite of fridge
and the opposite of midge
is antidisestablishmentarianism and bean.

The opposite of toe is kangaroo.
The opposite of nostril is kazoo.
The opposite of wood
and the opposite of good
is, no bout adoubt it, zoo and stew.

The opposite of someone else is me.
The opposite of skeleton is thee.
The opposite of crazy
and the opposite of lazy
is definitely us and maybe we.

Counting to a Billion

In the year 2000,
he started by counting fleas.

In the year 2001,
he fingered the bees.

In 2002, he checked
the number of leaves on the trees.

By 2003, he was down on his knees
adding up grains of sand.

In 2004, he asked
for a show of hands.

In the year 2005,
he counted the rain,

drop by drop
and didn't stop

till 2006,
when he itemized snow,

flake by flake
without a break

till 2007,
which he spent counting baked beans,

starting in Devon
and ending in Milton Keynes.

In the year 2008,
he totted up tears.

This took two years
and then, having made a mistake,

in 2010
he counted them all again.

In 2011,
he counted dogs;

in 2012,
he counted frogs.

In the year 2013,
he ticked off the birds in the sky.

In 2014,
he picked out the fish in the sea.

He counted balloons
in 2015

and in 2016
he counted spoons.

He counted mice
in 2017,

rats in 2018
and cats in 2019

and 2020,
which was plenty.

In the year 2021,
he counted eggs.

In the year 2022,
he reckoned up legs.

In 2023,
he took stock of stars

and in 2024
he counted some more

and again in 2025
and 2026.

By the end of 2027,
he'd finished with heaven.

In the year 2028,
he catalogued grapes.

In 2029
he tallied up bottles of wine –

and sipped from each one,
being thirsty.

In the year 2030,
he counted wasps.

In 2031,
he counted beetles.

In 2032,
he counted steeples.

In the year 2033,
he counted the dead,

but in 2034
there were more,

so, to count, in 2035,
you had to be alive.

In 2036,
he counted shops.

In 2037,
he counted ships.

In 2038,
he added up stones.

In 2039,
he tallied up phones.

In the year 2040,
he ran through mirrors.

In 2041,
he waded through rivers,

including brooks
and streams.

In 2042,
he counted books.

In 2043,
he counted dreams.

In 2044,
he numbered sheep.

In 2045,
he totalled hours spent asleep.

In 2046,
he added bricks.

In 2047,
he tallied sticks.

In 2048,
he counted children

and in 2049
he counted his millionth million.

By 2050 – BORED STIFF –
he'd reached a billion.

Please

Please.
Pretty please.
Pretty please with jam on top.
Pretty please with jam on top and ice-cream in the middle.

Please.
Beautiful please.
Beautiful please with a bunch of violets.
Beautiful please with a bunch of violets and a lollipop.

Please.
Gorgeous please.
Gorgeous please with perfume on.
Gorgeous please with perfume on and shiny shoes.

Please.
Lovely please.
Lovely please with silver wings.
Lovely please with silver wings and a magic wand.

46]

Please.
Handsome please.
Handsome please with violins.
Handsome please with violins and moonlight.

Please.
Bonny please.
Bonny please with cheese on top.
Bonny please with cheese on top and pickle in the middle.

Please.
Comely please.
Comely please with a marzipan pig.
Comely please with a marzipan pig and a sugar mouse.

Please.
Photogenic please.
Photogenic please with ribbons on.
Photogenic please with ribbons on and ruby earrings.

Please.
Prepossessing please.
Prepossessing please with stardust.
Prepossessing please with stardust and wishes.

Please.
Pulchritudinous please.
Pulchritudinous please with pizza.
Pulchritudinous please with pizza and fairy tales.

Pleeeeeeeeeeeeeeeeease.

Seven Deadly Adjectives

1 SLY

He was sly from birth, slithered out
without so much as a cry, lay in his crib,
slit-eyed, silent, sly.

Sleekit, too, as a toddler, kept a dummy
in his zipped lip twenty-four seven, kept
his nappies dry, sly;

slid about as a boy, listening, hearing
no good of himself, hung upside down
in his room like a bat, planning

his tit for tat, his take that; glid downstairs
in his stockinged feet, slipped from the house
like steam, teenaged, a sly moustache

under his nose. He liked being sly, loved it,
courted a sly girl, tall and slim, married her.
Sly twins came.

2 ARGUMENTATIVE

She'd argue black was white
to be right, that blue was red
to say the last word to be said,
that yellow was green, a king
was really a queen, that bright day
was night.

　　　　　She'd have it that
the long was the short of it,
the bottom line was only the tip
of the iceberg and fire was ice, insist
that the hill of a mole in the grass
was a mountain, the spill from a hole

in a glass was a fountain. She'd say
home was away, in out, truth doubt,
reason was madness, goodness badness,
argue the toss till heads were tails, peanuts
were huge rocks, small fry were giant whales
in the churning, quarrelling sea.

3 Selfish

He stashed his sweets in his sock drawer.
He hid his crisps in a bag on a hook on the wall.
He thought to himself – *Self's
eating them all.*

He kept his cakes in his satchel.
He locked crème brûlée in a box in a hole in the floor.
He promised himself – *Self's
having some more!*

He tucked his tuck in his cupboard.
He slid ice-cream behind books no one read on his shelf.
He smiled to himself – *Self's
seeing to self.*

He shut himself in his bedroom.
He got it all out, far away from everyone else.
It was spoiled, alas – exactly
like he was himself, himself, himself.

4 Moody

Those twins were moody, kept themselves
to themselves, hung out in the woods,
their faces sullen, their voices silent,
their hands muddy.

        They sat
at the back of the class at the same desk,
scowled at a shared book, sulked
when they stood up to read, mumbled,

sucked their milk through straws slowly
in a corner of the playground. They liked
the red-haired laughing boy with the ball,
followed him

        at a distance as he bounced
and kicked his way home. Those twins
carried on to the woods, stayed there till dusk,
not talking, digging their big hole.

5 Two-Faced

Two-faced, two-faced,
she had four eyes.
Two were brown under a black frown,
two were summery skies.

Two-faced, two-faced,
she'd a brace of noses.
One sniffed something fishy,
one roses.

Two-faced, two-faced,
she'd a double chin –
one fat,
t'other thin.

Two-faced, two-faced,
she had four ears.
Two heard only the boos of the crowd,
two heard the cheers.

Two-faced, two-faced,
she had four lips,
between their grins and grimaces
her forked-tongue slipped.

Two-faced, two-faced,
one face never slept,
one face snored in the darkness,
one face forever wept.

6 Boastful

He'd boast
he was best
if he played Beast
to Beauty.

He'd brag
in a brogue
he was Big
like it was a duty.

He'd bluff
till belief
floated off
like a pink balloon.

He'd strut
down the street
heading straight
for a fall – and soon.

7 LAZY

She had lazy, lazy bones.
She had stones in the shoes on her feet.
She had lazy, lazy, lazy bones.
She ignored the people she'd meet.

She had lazy, lazy blood.
She had mud in the nails of her hand.
She had lazy, lazy, lazy blood.
She never had anything planned.

She had lazy, lazy skin.
She had gums but no teeth in her grin.
She had lazy, lazy, lazy skin.
She wouldn't let anyone in.

She had lazy, lazy bones.
She slept under a blanket of earth.
O lazy, lazy, lazy bones,
how does death differ from birth?

The Theft

Like it or lump it, I stole a large egg
from a nest and humped it home
in my bag. Natural swag. My plan
was to pierce each end of the shell
with a pin then blow what was in
outside and if something died . . .
too bad. I was that kind of a lad.

Long story short – I left the egg
on a shelf in my room, took my eye
off the ball, and was woken at dawn,
four days on, by the *peck-peck-peck*
of a beak and the *skrek-skrek-skrek*
of a claw from the well-cracked egg.
Out came a leg, feathery limbs, a head.

Now, I had no name for the thing
that stood in my room, but it knew mine
and squawked it out in an eggy croak,
the last trace of yolk running down like tears
from its eye. And it lived for a year
in my bottom bunk till the room stank
and they left my scram on a tray in the corridor.

Came home one night – it was gone,
the window flung, and a big yellow moon
like an egg in a non-stick pan outside.

I was sad, glad, felt bad – but not for long.
And if I could write, the story I'd tell is this.
And if I could sing, then this would be
my song. Don't steal, kids. It ain't worth it.

Lost

Left, left again, right, left, right, right again then left,
up, down, around and about, in, out, right, left, right . . .
Excellent, I'm lost; all alone on the lip of a wood –
sip, slurp, it's sucked me in, a morsel of white bread
in its dark cheek. The trees

                              are breathing quietly.
Who knows if a witch isn't a heap of leaves and old twigs,
hunched and sleeping under a bush? Or a bird
wasn't a girl like me, put under a spell and made to sing
on the branches of a silver birch

                                    till another girl came
to take her place? I run away through the woods,
all voices miles away now. Who knows that a stone
isn't a toad with a jewel in its brain that hops away
when you touch it? Or a log isn't a sleeping prince

who'll suddenly stand, shaking the bugs and beetles
from his rusty hair? Lost is thrilling, my own scream
swooping away into the heart of this wood
as the night comes down, down, over my eyes
like a blindfold.

Jamjar

A girl in her garden peeped into a jamjar and fell inside.
She passed a wasp as she fell, it was licking
a smear of strawberry jam from the rim of the jar.
How far is the bottom? she cried as she fell.
Far, very far, drawled the wasp, *terribly far.*

Down she fell. The jar was a bell and her scream
was its tinkly, echoing ring. A green caterpillar
crawled up the outside glass of the jar, blinked
with its bulging alien eyes. *Help!* screeched the girl.
   Help!
Alas, it lisped, *there's no help in the whole wide world.*

On she hurled, into the well of the jar, till the opening
was a tiny star and dandelion clocks were silver planets
spinning in space. A spider hung from a thread
and peered at her face. *Throw me a rope!* she begged.
Not here, not now, it sneered, *nor any time or place.*

Bump. The jamjar's floor was snow and ice, stretching
for freezing miles. The girl skated away, all alone,
calling for home. White wolves ran in her tracks
under the hard stars. *Show me the way,* she sobbed.
No way to show, they howled, *and no way back.*

Then a hand picked up the jar; a mean squint eye swam
like a needlefish to the glass; poisonous breath clouded
    it over.
This will do for a vase, said a spiteful voice, as a Witch
filled up the jamjar with water, then stared in amazed,
glee in her eyes, at her swimming and brand new creature.

The Giantess

Where can I find seven small girls to be pets,
where can I find them?
One to comb the long grass of my hair
with this golden rake,
one to dig with this copper spade
the dirt from under my nails.
I will pay them in crab-apples.

Where can I find seven small girls to help me,
where can I find them?
A third to scrub at my tombstone teeth
with this mop in its bronze bucket,
a fourth to scoop out the wax from my ears
with this platinum trowel.
I will pay them in yellow pears.

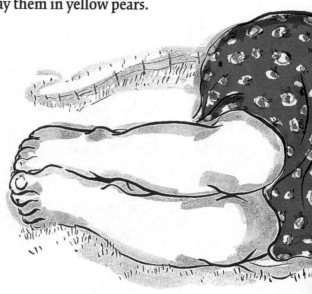

Where can I find seven small girls to be good dears,
where can I find them?
A fifth one to clip the nails of my toes
with these sharp silver shears,
a sixth to blow my enormous nose
with this satin sheet.
I will pay them in plums.

But the seventh girl will stand on the palm of my hand,
singing and dancing,
and I will love the tiny music of her voice,
her sweet little jigs.
I will pay her in grapes and kumquats and figs.
Where can I find her?
Where can I find seven small girls to be pets?

The Written Queen

I stare through my window.
The Written Queen stands outside
in the rain in her green robes,
tall as a tree, sad as the dripping leaves.
She is waiting for me.

I go to sleep. The Written Queen
breathes in the dark room,
soft as shade, hushed, black
as a closed and dreaming eye.
She is watching me.

I go out, pass under
the curtseying trees, the doffed clouds,
and see the Written Queen
at the end of the avenue.
She is beckoning me.

I read – her hand's shadow
falls on the words of my book.
I dance – her tapping shoe
follows the curves of my foot.
She is devoted to me.

I take up paper and pen
and write her, line by line, once
upon a time. Here is her sceptre, her crown,
her palace, here is her throne.
She is all mine.

A Week as My Home Town

Monday:

Rain. I'm the Library, round-shouldered, my stone brow
frowning at pigeons, my windows steamed up
like spectacles, my swing doors tut-tutting, my bricks
beginning to feel the damp.

                    Readers come,
whispering and coughing, shaking umbrellas
at the back of my yawning marble throat. My old lifts sigh
up and down, up and down, up and down. *Ssssshhh.*

Books flap in my head like birds.

Tuesday:

Weak sun. I'm the Park. My trees
wear last night's rain like jewels.
I shake birds from my hair as I wake, gargle
with a water-fountain, admire my green face
in the mirror of a small lake.

                My thoughts
are a game of bowls, slow and calm.
I hum to myself in a lawnmower bass
among my bright municipal flowers,
my namesake benches.

Wednesday:

Fog. Museum, me. I hark back
to the past for endless hours, hoard
bronze coins in glass wallets, keep
long-gone summer butterflies on pins.

I remember things, pick
over old bones, look under cold stones,
check the names of the Kings and Queens
who sat on the gold thrones.

My stained-glass eyes stare inwards.

Thursday:

Sunshine, I'm the Main Road.
I lie on my back, stretch out
my side-street arms, wriggle
my alley toes, my mews fingers.

My throat is a tunnel
under a river. I burp cars
into the sparkling daylight,
belch lorries and juggernauts.

My heart's a roundabout,
in love with the next town.

Friday:

Grey cloud. I'm the Cinema, daydream
all day, can't sleep at night, hear

voices . . . *to infinity and beyond* . . . see
faces . . . *I'm all aloooone* . . . smell

popcorn . . . *please sir, can I have
some more* . . . They shine a light

in my eyes, prod at my plush red teeth.
I want to phone home. I'll be right here.

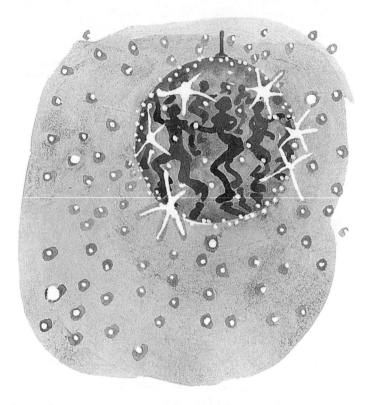

Saturday:

Frost. I'm the Disco. My neon lips
pout at the shivery night. My heart thumps
so loud the queue outside can hear it.

I wear light, glitterballs, lasers, strobe,
too much perfume. One day I'll give up smoking.
If anyone asks if I'm dancing, I'm dancing.

Sunday:

Snow. I'm the Church,
stone-flags for my shoes,
for my hat a steeple.

I kneel by the side of the graves
and sob with my bells.
Where are the people?

Fine Weather

The dead like fine weather, their cold bones
grow warm in the soil, under the daffodils,
the tulips, the roses, under the heather.

The dead enjoy sunshine, their pale skulls
are new-laid eggs in the ground, their coffins
brown as toast. The dead love summer most –

when the living come, in dresses or shirt-sleeves,
to picnic by their graves. The dead relax, bask,
as sunlight heals their stones, their dates, their names.

Deal with It

I saw some graffiti, it read
R.I.P. . . . Elvis is dead,
and though I think with my head,
I believe with my heart, grieve with it.
Elvis was King and I never heard him sing.

I saw a headline, it led
Elvis's death – pics of it,
and though I plan with my head,
I risk with my heart, wish with it.
Elvis could move and I never saw him groove.

I saw a badge, it said
Elvis is dead – deal with it,
and though I judge with my head,
I give with my heart, love with it.
Elvis lived and I never heard him live.